MW00899234

Coconut Oil Nutrition Book

30 Coconut Oil Recipes and 130 Applications for Weight Loss, Hair Loss, Beauty and Health

By

Patrick Smith

Copyright © 2014 Patrick Smith

All rights reserved.

ISBN-10: 1500396389
ISBN-13: 978-1500396381

Contents

Introduction:
The Secret of Our Ancestors

When I was ten years old, I met a man who told me something that would change the way I thought about nutrition forever. His name was Malin and he was born on a small atoll somewhere in the South Pacific.

However, that's not where I met him. I was on vacation in Italy at the time, sunning on a beach with the rest of my family. It was midday and we were surrounded by hundreds of other tourists. Suddenly, I heard a man calling out from afar.

I turned and noticed a dark skinned body, leaner and stronger than I had ever seen. But he was no bodybuilder. Interested, I observed him for a while. He was walking along the beach, going from one parasol to the next, carrying a basket filled with coconuts that he was trying to sell. I remember being fascinated, because it was the first time that I had seen this exotic fruit. Until then I only knew about coconuts from cartoons and as a flavor for chocolate bars.

When Malin arrived at our parasol, he offered us cut coconut pieces. He said that coconuts were extremely healthy and that his people had known this for a thousand years. My dad, however, was reading his newspaper and waved him away.

I immediately felt drawn to follow this man.

See, my dad and the rest of my family were overweight, while Malin looked as if Michelangelo's David was actually a statue of *him*. I wanted to know that secret his people had known for so many years. Having grown up in a family that knew nothing about nutrition, it wasn't surprising that I was chubby myself.

I quickly ran after Malin. When I eventually caught up with him I asked him to tell me about his people. We spent hours roaming the beach together, selling and eating coconuts. I will never forget the things he told me.

Like Malin, the other islanders living in the Pacific all look like athletes. Health issues like obesity, heart disease, liver disease and diabetes are unheard of among them. He said it was not due to something special they did or had, because the same was true for Eskimos and other people that live outside of modern society. He also believed it wasn't their natural exercise of fishing every day, as this only made them strong. Being muscular and healthy are not the same thing. There is, however, one characteristic that all wild living people share: They eat natural, unprocessed foods.

Malin was a member of the Tokelauan people, who get most of their daily calories from coconuts, which consist to 90% of saturated fats. These people are the biggest consumers of saturated fats in the world. Perhaps this strikes you as odd. We are told that saturated fats cause a lot of health problems, especially heart conditions, yet it turns out that Malin's people eat more saturated fat than the average American.

The same is true for Eskimos. They eat not only more fat than the average American, but also more meat. That is because they mainly eat whales and fish, and the outermost skin of a whale is a fatty substance called blubber.

How is it that we get these health issues and they don't?

The reason is the way our food is produced. All of our processed foods contain various chemicals and so-called trans fats, which have been linked to heart disease long ago. Trans fats are uncommon in nature, but are created artificially. The processed foods of our modern civilization are poisoned with these trans fats and many different kinds of chemicals.

But it gets worse. Did you know that plastic residues have been found in our bloodstreams? Everything that comes in contact with plastic inevitably has plastic molecules sticking to it, which we then ingest. In fact, our bodies are so filled with pollutants that it is not even good for the ground, if we rot in it after death. This is how much we have poisoned ourselves.

The difference between the wild living people and modern people is that we no longer eat natural foods. We cook and process our milk instead of drinking it fresh and we feed our cattle with corn instead of grass, even though the stomach of a cow is not able to deal with it.

Do you know what happens if a cow is given corn? First of all, the cow doesn't even want to eat it, so the animal is pumped full of growth hormones to make it insanely hungry. Only now will it eat the corn. But as I said, a cow is not meant to eat it. The corn causes the cow's stomach to be so acidic that it becomes a cauldron of bacterial growth. The animal then has to be pumped full of antibiotics to ensure it won't perish from a bacterial infection. This is the animal that we then eat.

Surely, you see the problem. Our intuition should tells us that this can't be good for us. We know this is not the way we should consume meat. This is the difference between the normal meat you can buy in the shops and organic meat from free ranging cows that only eat grass. The reason cows are treated this way is that it makes the animal grow very fast, which means it enables a higher meat production rate, more meat to sell and hence more profit. But we either pay our doctors or our farmers.

Humans used to live in the wild, and our bodies are built so survive on the foods provided by nature. Only when the industrial age began, these modern diseases of civilization started to appear. They are symptoms of our industries, of our processing, of the use of trans fats and chemicals that are now residing within us.

It is not that coconuts are miracle foods, as they are often hyped up to be. Yes, they do have a wide range of applications and are indeed very healthy, but their main benefit is the simple fact that they are a natural, typically unprocessed food. Coconut oil, which is extracted from white coconut meat, has the very same benefit.

Therefore, it is an essential ingredient in any kitchen. Replacing butter and margarine with coconut oil already makes a big difference.

In this book, I discuss what I've learned about coconut oil in my adult life, while pouring through scientific research and through self-experimentation. I explain how I use coconut oil and how you can use it as well. There are hundreds of ways it can improve your health and find its way on your plate. It is a versatile friend and can even serve as body lotion and hair conditioner.

Let's go and find out more!

Chapter 1: A Villain Turned Hero

Not too long ago, I saw a doctor on television commenting on the current revival of coconut oil in the world of health. He told people that coconut oil is a hype and actually bad for your health, because it contains more saturated fats than butter, lard or beef.

He was wrong.

There is a misconception regarding the healthiness of coconuts that can be traced back to the 1990s. At the time, scientific research seemed to suggest that coconuts are fat monsters that clog your arteries and lead to heart disease, even more than eating the greasiest hamburgers imaginable. Clearly, this resulted in coconuts getting a very bad reputation.

Still, the people of Polynesia, like my friend Malin from the Tokelauans in the South Pacific, swear by this food. As I said in the introduction, they get most of their calories from coconuts and eat more saturated fats than anyone else in the world, all from coconut meat. Why is there such a mismatch between what some doctors say, what research used to show and what the Polynesians have been doing for a thousand years?

It turns out that by reviewing the scientific literature of the nineties, one finds that most of the old studies were done with partially hydrogenated (processed) coconut oil. The researchers did this because they needed to artificially raise the cholesterol levels of their lab animals (rabbits) to collect certain data. In other words, the scientists gave their rabbits processed coconut oil to intentionally raise their cholesterol levels. From this it was concluded that coconut oil was bad for the heart.

The process of hydrogenation in what we know as "processed foods" is a mechanism that creates trans fats, which are known to clog arteries and cause heart attacks. It also destroys a large percentage of the antioxidants, essential fatty acids and other healthy nutrients found in unprocessed coconuts. Basically, by giving hydrogenated coconut oil to their lab animals, the scientists in the nineties simply found one more piece of evidence for how bad trans fats and processed foods are. It had nothing to do with coconuts themselves.

Sometimes, a research result gets out of hand, enters the public domain and becomes a national game of telephone, distorting and generalizing the information.

Virgin, organic, non-hydrogenated coconut oil (the normal coconut oil you can buy) is the exact opposite of what its reputation made it out to be.

A lot of new research has been done to assess the health benefits of coconuts in the past two decades and it turns out they are among the healthiest foods available on planet earth. It is just as the Polynesians had always known.

Not everybody has caught up with this new information, which is why some doctors and even whole organizations still incorrectly warn people against eating coconuts and the oils extracted from them. Yes, coconut oil contains 90% saturated fats, but they don't harm you. Different types of saturated fats behave in different ways. I talk more about this issue at the end of chapter 3.

There are two groups of people that have been working to give coconuts the good, new image they deserve. One of them is the scientific community involved in the medical research that showed coconuts are a good and healthy food. The other group is comprised of vegetarians and vegans, given that the natural coconut fat is sweet, nutritious and a perfect replacement for butter and margarine.

Vegans in particular like to use it for cooking and baking, because it has the consistency of margarine at room temperature and melts into a liquid above 75°F or 24°C. It can easily be used to make cupcakes and cake crusts that come with a natural coconut flavor and fragrance.

Personally, I use coconut oil in the same way. It is what I use for butter, not only for bread but for baking and frying. I especially like sautéing onions, vegetables and other ingredients, because they drink in the flavor of the oil and make any dish a completely new experience.

Movie theaters have been using coconut oil for their popcorn for a long time, even back in the nineties when coconuts got their bad reputation. With this in mind, I've tried making popcorn using coconut oil myself and found that movie theaters did the right thing for all those years. There can be no better way to eat popcorn than this.

With the health benefits on one side and the versatility and flavor on the other side, coconut oil has become the sweetheart of the natural foods movement. The villain from the nineties turned out to be a hero.

Chapter 2: Dosage and Types of Coconut Oil

Dosage of Coconut Oil

As I explained in the last chapter, health organizations and some individuals still warn of eating coconut oil. I also told you that it is due to the fact that coconut oil used to have an incorrect bad reputation due to some problematic studies in the nineties.

However, these warnings are not always wrong, because they often simply say that *high intake* of coconut oil is bad for you. This is correct, of course, because even healthy foods can and will be unhealthy if you eat too much of them. It is a general rule and important to keep in mind. Even breathing too much oxygen has its consequences (hyperventilation).

A few years ago, a friend of mine wanted to be healthier and started taking vitamins. Foolishly, he believed this was the key to health. As you can imagine, he overdid it and took way too many vitamins than the human body can handle. Because of this, he developed a number of conditions. His mind became slow and dull, he was tired all day and he had trouble concentrating even on something as simple as reading a newspaper article. It took several months for him to return to normal.

Give your body what it needs and can use, but not more than that. Never make the mistake my friend made. Never overuse coconut oil or any other substance, thinking more of it will also benefit you more.

When I first started using coconut oil, I wasn't sure how much was good and how much was overindulgent. Generally, if you replace your butter and margarine with it, then you are fine. I have done a lot of research on coconut oil and have read many scientific journals to figure out how much I should eat.

The recommended daily intake of virgin coconut oil is: 1/2 tablespoon per 25 pounds (about 11 kilograms) of body mass. The first 25 pounds count twice.

For example, if you were to weigh 50 pounds, the recommended daily dosage would be 1 + 1/2 tbs. If you weigh 75 pounds, it is 1 + 1/2 + 1/2 = 2 tbs. This is an easy rule to remember.

Here is an overview of body mass versus the recommended daily dosage:

25 pounds / 11 kg – 1 tablespoon

50 pounds / 22 kg – 1.5 tablespoons

75 pounds / 34 kg – 2 tablespoons

100 pounds / 45 kg – 2.5 tablespoons

125 pounds / 56 kg – 3 tablespoons

150 pounds / 68 kg – 3.5 tablespoons

175 pounds / 79 kg – 4 tablespoons

You should not go above that to make sure you don't overdo it.

Types of Coconut Oil

Pure Coconut Oil

This type of coconut oil is extracted from dried coconut flakes, known as copra. It is unrefined, contains no additives of any kind and is mainly extracted by compression of copra in a mill. As we will see, it has a large number of uses, such as cosmetics, medicine, food, serving as massaging oil and hair oil.

Virgin Coconut Oil

Also known as "unrefined coconut oil", this variety is made from fresh coconuts. It is natural and almost not processed with heat or chemicals of any kind. Apart from the obvious health benefits of non-chemically processed food, it also has a mild coconut taste and smell, which I describe as somewhat nutty. On top of that, virgin coconut oil has a high nutritional value. Since it loses some of its nutritional value during processing, refined coconut oil is slightly inferior to the virgin variety.

An extra benefit of virgin coconut oil is the fact that its natural taste makes it an alternative for parfait. Fresh bread and virgin coconut oil is more than bread and butter, so you can save money by saving on parfait, salami, cheese or whatever and lose weight in the process.

Refined Coconut Oil (RBD)

Many manufacturers of coconut oil don't use the fresh fruit but the copra in order to produce the oil. This copra then goes on to be refined, bleached and deodorized, which is why this type of coconut oil is also abbreviated as RBD. The final product is a white oil without any taste and odor, which is how you can distinguish refined from unrefined coconut oil very easily.

The refining typically uses a chemical distillation process that depends on lye or other harsh solvents. While this process causes the oil to lose some of its healthy properties, refined coconut oil is still almost as nutritious as unrefined (virgin) coconut oil. If the natural coconut taste of the virgin oil bothers you, then you should definitely go for this one. That, however, means it won't be able to serve you as a tasty alternative to parfait, which I find to be a key benefit of virgin coconut oil.

Fractionated Coconut Oil

Manufacturers of this coconut oil lower its melting point in order to make it usable in liquid form. This is done by removing the long-chained fatty acids and medium-chain lauric acids, leaving only the capric and caprylic acid. Fractioned coconut oil finds application in soaps, skin-care lotions, creams and other products that soften and relax the skin. It is also used in medicines, in massage oil blends, vitamins and actives and as a carrier for essential oils. Since it is stripped of the long-chained fatty acids and lauric acids, it is not meant for consumption.

Cold-Pressed, Expeller-Pressed and Centrifuged Oil

When I first saw these terms, I thought I was dealing with different types of coconut oils. However, they are simply names for various ways of extracting the oil from dry or fresh coconuts and can be found in both virgin and refined coconut oil.

Organic and Organic Virgin Coconut Oil

A coconut oil is considered to be *organic*, if it is extracted from coconuts raised on organic manure and if no fertilizers, insecticides and other chemicals have been used. This makes it the healthiest variety of coconut oil available. It finds use in thousands of cosmetic products, like organic creams, lotions and soaps. If virgin coconut oil is produced from organic coconuts, it is referred to as "organic virgin coconut oil".

You can recognize organic coconut oil by its certification, usually given by either one of these organizations:

NOP – European Organic Regulation

JAS – Export Certificates for Japan

GOTZS – Global Organic Textile Standards

USDA – National Organic Program

NPOP – Indian National Program for Organic Production

CAAQ – Quebec Organic Reference Standard

ECOCERT

Bio Suisse Standards

IOFAM Basic Standards.

Chapter 3:
Buying and Storing Coconut Oil

Since there are several types of coconut oil, you are probably wondering which one you should use. Fortunately, this is very easy to answer. It all depends on what you want to use it for. Coconut oil has a large number of applications, from weight loss to hair care and even massaging. Here is a list of what I recommend for different uses.

Purpose – Recommended Coconut Oil

Weight Loss – Virgin

Cooking and Frying – Refined

Health – Organic, Virgin

Hair and Skin Care – Pure, Unrefined

Medicinal uses – Virgin, Organic

Massage Oil – Pure, Unrefined

An easy to remember rule of thumb is that refined coconut oil is very hygienic and thus good for cooking / eating. On the other hand, unrefined oils (which includes pure oils) are perfect for applications outside of your body, such as a massage oil, hair and skin care.

Where To Buy Coconut Oil

Nowadays, coconut oil (especially refined and pure) is available in many grocery stores. In tropical countries that actually *produce* coconut oil, it can be bought nearly everywhere.

For places like Europe, the US and Canada, you should be able to find coconut oil in larger grocery stores, drug stores or department stores. One way to find all the different varieties of coconut oil is to check out stores in areas of your city that are home to people from other countries. Just like you can get outstanding Asian food in China town, you can get coconut oil in places with people from India, the Philippines, Sri Lanka, Thailand and Africa.

Last but not least, the Internet is your friend. You can get coconut oil from Amazon and many other online shops.

If you go on holiday to places like the Philippines, Thailand, coastal India or other countries that produce coconut oil, you can buy it from someone local. In these countries coconut oil is everywhere, so even villages have at least one person extracting it. I always thought it quite a treat to get the product right where it is made.

What to Look Out for When Buying Coconut Oil

It does not matter which brand you buy. I have never come across a bad product. Coconut oil is a very common substance in many tropical countries and its production is a well-oiled machine that looks back on decades of experience.

However, if you buy coconut oil in large amounts, make sure to check the manufacturing date and shelf life. Generally, you are safe in this regard, because coconut oil has a long shelf life of more than a year, if it remains unopened. Still, if you deal with large amounts, the fresher you can get it the better.

The one thing you really want to look out for is the price. When it comes to coconut oil, prices differ quite a lot and can go fairly high. This is due to the high quality and demand of this product as more and more people become aware of its benefits.

In my experience, refined coconut oil is the cheapest, which is good since you can use it for cooking. It is followed by virgin and organic oils on second place. Third place goes to fractionated coconut oil. Naturally, if you buy in bulk you get it cheaper.

Buying in bulk is not only cheaper, but you also have to search less often to find it. Since coconut oil has such a long shelf life, you can safely buy some for several months in advance. Just make sure you test it before you buy a particular kind, so you are sure that you like its taste (or lack of it). Don't buy *too* much in advance, because despite its shelf life, the best results are still achieved with a fresh product.

Storing Coconut Oil

One of the things that I just love about coconut oil is that it doesn't need to be kept in the fridge like butter or margarine. If you put it in the fridge, it actually gets as hard as wax and can't be put it on bread for quite a while, but in your hand, it instantly melts into a liquid akin to olive oil. So if your intention is to only cook and fry with it, you can put it in the fridge, but if you want to use it on bread, you need to keep it at room temperature.

Chapter 4:
An Overview of Health Benefits

Coconut oil is often hyped as a super food and a large number of health benefits are attributed to it. However, like all foods, coconuts and their oils are only ingredients. It is not a magic potion that will cure all your ailments.

As I like to say, "Don't go on a diet, instead have a good diet."

This simply means that a super food or magic bullet diet won't get the pounds rolling. Don't force your body through periods of eating little. Eat natural, healthy foods instead. Coconut oil is such a food. It doesn't *heal* you, it only *helps* you, like all good ingredients. If you replace butter and especially margarine with coconut oil, it will already be good for you.

Let's have a look at some of the effects that coconut oil has on your health.

Anti-inflammatory: Research suggests that coconut oil can help to suppress inflammations and assist the body in repairing tissue. Did you know that clinical depression is an inflammatory disease? Because of this, coconut oil may very well offer some relief of this condition.

Anti-viral: Coconut oil has antiviral properties, which means it can help to kill viruses that cause many conditions, such as herpes, influenza, measles, hepatitis C, SARS and so on.

Anti-microbial: Coconut oil contains the same medium-chain fatty acids and monoglycerides that are also found in the milk of any female mammal, including humans. Like all things in nature, there is a good reason why it is this way. Mammals produce milk with these ingredients, because they show antimicrobial properties and are thus good for an infant. These acids and monoglycerides disrupt the lipid structures of microbes and shut them down. In addition, coconut oil contains large quantities of lauric acid. Both this and the other fatty acids in coconut oil help to protect against infection from bacteria, viruses, yeast, fungi and parasites. Beneficial bacteria in our gut are not negatively affected by coconut oil, so there are no negative side effects to its anti-microbial property.

Anti-carcinogenic: Coconut oil has antimicrobial properties, so it helps to prevent the spread of cancer cells and enhances the immune system.

Anti-fungal: It assists the body to kill fungi and yeast that can cause infections.

Antioxidant: It protects against the formation of free-radicals and the damage they can cause.

Anti-protozoa: It helps to kill giardia, a common protozoan infection of the gut.

Anti-bacterial: It kills bacteria that cause throat infections, ulcers, urinary tract infections, gum diseases and many other bacterial infections.

Anti-parasitic: It helps to rid your body of parasites, such as lice, tapeworms and others.

Nutrient absorption: Since coconut oil is easily digestible, it doesn't require your stomach to work so much.

Now let's have a look at a few practical applications.

Skin Care

When I first started using coconut oil, I did not know much about its fantastic versatility with regards to skin- and hair care. Coconut oil is solid if it's cold and much like margarine at room temperature. In your hand, it melts into an oil that can be used as lotion and serves as a natural moisturizer.

If you suffer from dry skin, coconut oil acts like a mineral oil, but without any side effects. My mother used to have extremely dry hands and her skin would flake and hurt. I told her about coconut oil and gave her a jar, which she promptly used for her hands and has been ever since.

Coconut oil is a safe, natural solution for this kind of problem and it even comes with a coconut smell. Research suggests that it also helps to suppress premature aging, wrinkles and sagging of the skin, yet it is much cheaper than skin care products. In fact, coconut oil is an ingredient in many lotions, soaps and creams, which clearly shows its worth.

Another way to use coconut oil is the treatment of skin ailments such as infections, eczemas, psoriasis and dermatitis. My youngest sibling suffers from atopic eczema. It causes his skin to itch, so he tends to scratch it bloody. We have successfully used coconut oil to keep the itching in check.

Hair Care

The health of your hair has a big impact on its own and your overall appearance. It is something that I take very seriously and try to improve whenever I can.

Hair and skin both have a protective layer of fat that is removed every time you take a shower. Skin can regenerate its protective fat quickly, but hair needs a day or two for that, which means a clean person is also a person with unshielded hair. Obviously, this is a problem.

I recently read a research paper that talked about the effects of using coconut oil on your hair *before* washing it. It turns out that doing so is one of the best protections against the loss of proteins while washing your hair. I've been doing it ever since, over a month now and I noticed that my hair has more volume and strength than before.

Every time you wash and lose proteins, your hair is weakened and has to reproduce them. It's been a long time since I used hair products. Coconut oil is pretty much all I use today, both before and after washing. It works as a conditioner, gives nutrients to the hair, allows for damaged hair to regrow and protects if from combing damage. At the same time, it makes the hair shiny.

Because of all these and many more qualities, coconut oil is the main substance used for hair care in India. People use it on a daily basis after bathing or showering. In those countries where coconut oil is a normal ingredient in foods, practices like this are normal as well. The benefits of coconut oil for skin and hair care is an ancestral knowledge to these people that has been passed down through generations.

Weight Loss and Heart Health

Because of the faulty studies on coconut oil in the nineties, there is still a lot of misinformation out there. Many people will say that coconut oil is unhealthy due to its large content of saturated fats. Everybody knows that saturated fats are bad for the heart, but as always, reality is more complicated than such a general rule. There are different kinds of saturated fats, some of which are good and some of which are bad for your health.

Remember my Tokelauan friend, Malin, who I talked about in the introduction. I told you that his people get most of their calories from coconuts, which contain 90% saturated fats. Yet these islanders are the poster children for health. They know nothing of obesity and all those other diseases of modern civilization, despite eating more saturated fats than anyone else in the world.

What makes their fats different from the ones we are eating every day?

A molecule of fat has the form of a chain. Based on the number of carbon atoms such a molecule contains, it is classified either as a short-, medium- or long-chained fat. Most of the saturated fats in coconut meat are in the category of short- and medium-chain fats. Both of these can be absorbed by the liver directly and without complication.

Long-chained fatty acids, on the other hand, need some time before the body can absorb them and use their energy content. Because of this difference, shorter chains are more easily digestible and are turned into energy quickly, making them less likely to be stored in your body. The types of fatty acids in coconut and many other unprocessed foods don't add to obesity and are not the harmful kind found in vegetable oils.

Due to its digestibility, coconut oil increases the metabolic rate and decreases stress on the pancreas. Energy is produced more quickly and efficiently, which tells the brain that less food is required to meet the daily energy need. This starts to get the pounds rolling, because the shorter fatty acids are used, not stored. Losing those extra pounds is one piece of the puzzle that decreases the risk of suffering a heart attack.

As mentioned before, coconut meat also contains large quantities of lauric acid, which (among others) prevents high cholesterol levels and blood pressure. Obviously, this also benefits the health of your heart.

Many More Benefits

I've decided to write about the above topics to give you a clear idea as to how coconut oil and its contents are good for your health. I also want you to see in what kind of ways coconut oil can be used other than just eating it.

There is, however, a long list of things it can be used for. If I were to write a few paragraphs on each of these applications, this would be a stupendously long and boring book to read and many things would be mentioned over and over again.

Therefore, in the final chapter of this book, I have assembled concise list of 130 applications and uses of coconut oil from which you can pick and choose. I have not used all of them myself, because some of them deal with health issues that don't apply to me. They all, however, stem from the scientific papers I poured through while doing my research on coconut oil. Many of those papers can be found in the appendix at the end of this book.

Before we get to the list, I first want to give you some of the recipes that I like and use a lot.

Chapter 5: 30 Coconut Oil Recipes

The following recipes are among those I use and enjoy myself, but there are infinite possibilities of using coconut oil in food. For example, you can simply replace butter with it and immediately use any recipe you know, this time with coconut flavor and its benefits.

In the list below, I don't give calorie counts. Here is why: First, it depends hugely on the exact amounts of coconut oil being used, because it is very high in calories. Since everybody uses a slightly different amount, that is everybody fills teaspoons with more or less oil, giving a calorie count would be incorrect, anyway.

Secondly, you don't need to watch your calories. I used to track every single one of them once, but it is just a pain and wastes your time. If you eat good, healthy foods and don't overeat (stop when you're done, not when the plate is empty), then you will be fine. Only people who don't eat well, or want to eat unhealthy foods in-between healthy ones, need to track their calories.

Breakfasts and Snacks

1. Banana Coconut Crêpe

Bananas are another healthy food you should adopt, if you're not eating it already. This is a breakfast even banana haters cannot resist.

2 **eggs**
¼ cup **coconut** or **dairy yogurt**
1 cup warm **water**
½ cup **flour** of your choice
½ tbs **panela** (optional)
1 tbs of melted **coconut oil** for cooking
A pinch of **salt**
A dash of **cinnamon**
4-6 **bananas**

Combine yogurt, water and flour in a blender until it is smooth. Cover it and let it soak overnight. In the morning, add eggs, panela, 1 tbs of melted coconut oil, salt and cinnamon to the mix and blend it again until it is smooth. This is going to be your crêpe batter.

Heat a frying pan over medium heat and spread a layer of coconut oil over the pan. You can do this either by moving the pan or using a pastry brush. Once the pan is hot, pour 2-3 tbs of the crêpe batter into it and spread it into a circle. After frying it for 2 minutes, use a spatula to loosen the edges of the crêpe and carefully flip it over. Fry the other side for 1 more minute before taking it out of the pan. Repeat this process until the batter is used up. Don't forget to keep the pan oiled up.

Finally, roll each crêpe around a banana. Optionally, you can try spreading apple sauce on the crêpes before rolling them around the bananas.

Enjoy!

2. Oat Bran Coconut Muffins

These muffins are on my table almost every weekend, much to the delight to friends coming over. I usually use mini muffin tins, which yields about 40 muffins with the following recipe. If regular muffin tins are used, it should be enough for about a dozen muffins.

2 ½ cups uncooked **oat bran**
2 tbs **baking powder**
1-2 tbs **salt**
2/3 cup **vegetable glycerin** (or another liquid sweetener of your choice)
¾ cup **water**
2 tbs **cinnamon**
2 **eggs**
2 tbs **vanilla extract** (optional)
4 tbs **coconut oil**
optionally, add some **nuts** (cashews are a healthy choice)

Preheat your oven to 425°F / 220°C.

Mix all dry and wet ingredients together in separate bowls.

Add wet to dry ingredients and add nuts if you are using them.

You can either put the mix into greased muffin tins or place it on a prepared cookie sheet or baking stone.

Bake it for 10-20 minutes until the centers of your muffins are well set.

Enjoy!

3. Coconut Flour Zucchini

This is a family favorite, especially since it combines two healthy foods and is quickly done in 18-20 minutes.

2-4 tsp **coconut oil**
2 **eggs** (beaten)
2 cups **zucchini** (sliced)
1/2 cup **coconut flour**
1/2 cup **parmesan cheese** (optional, grated)
1 tsp salt

First, add coconut oil to your favorite frying pan and heat it at about 375°F (190°C).

Add two eggs to a bowl and lightly beat them.

Mix coconut flour, salt and optionally Parmesan cheese in a second bowl.

Slice a zucchini and dip the slices into the beaten egg, then place them in the flour mix to coat them with it.

Put the zucchini in the frying pan and fry them until they are golden brown. It takes 2-4 minutes for each side

Put the fried zucchini on a plate and serve them immediately.

Enjoy!

Note: Works better with the Parmesan, but it is healthier without. We like both alternatives. Also, we use organic eggs.

4. Fried Coconut Tomatoes

This is very simple tomato recipe I make at least once a week in the morning. It can be used for tomatoes of any color: green, red, or orange.

¼ tsp **salt**
¼ tsp **pepper**
½ cup **coconut flour**
1 **egg** (lightly beaten)
¼ tsp **paprika** (optional)
1 large **tomato** (sliced)
2-4 tsp **coconut oil**

Put the coconut oil into a frying pan and heat it over medium-high heat.

Mix the salt, pepper, optional paprika, coconut flour in a shallow bowl.

Add an egg to another bowl and lightly beat it.

Slice the tomato and dip the slices into the egg, then into the coconut flour mixture.

Fry the dipped slices in the pan, 2-3 minutes on each side.

Serve immediately and enjoy!

5. Coconut Popcorn

I'm a health nut, but I love the occasional popcorn. Whenever I watch a movie with my family or friends, there is only 1 kind of popcorn that can go along with it. This one made me a legendary popcorn maker in my circle and it is an old movie theater secret.

3 tbs **coconut oil**
½ cup **popcorn**
3 tbs **coconut butter** (optional)
Salt

Put the coconut oil into a frying pan and heat it over medium-high heat. You can also use a wok for this, which works even better.

Add popcorn and cover the pan or wok with the lid slightly ajar for steam to escape.

Melt coconut butter in a small saucepan. You can also use regular butter, which changes the flavor and is very good, but less healthy. Once the butter gets a slightly brow color, the flavor has reached its peak.

Once the popcorn is done, turn the heat down to the lowest setting. Pour 1/3 of the melted butter over the popcorn, sprinkle with salt and stir the mix. Repeat this process until the butter is used up.

Optionally, leave the pan or wok on the lowest heat for 5-10 more minutes to rid the popcorn of moisture inside. This makes the crunchiest popcorn possible. The first time you do this, I suggest to do this only with a part of the popcorn to practice and compare both options.

6. Blueberry Banana Coco-Muffins

These are some of my favorite muffin recipes, handed to me by my grandma, changed slightly to incorporate coconut, which made it even better.

½ cup unrefined **coconut oil**
½ cup **honey** (or less, if you wish to limit sweets)
¾ tsp **sea salt**
6 **eggs**
1 ½ tsp **vanilla extract**
½ tsp **almond extract**
¾ cup **coconut flour**
1 **banana** (mashed)
1 cup frozen or fresh **blueberries**
paper cups for the muffins

Melt the coconut oil in a small saucepan over low heat. Then turn off the heat and let it cool a bit.

While the oil is melting, use a whisk or mixer to blend the eggs, salt, vanilla and almond extract in a big bowl.

Add the honey to the cooling coconut oil and stir it slightly. Pour this liquid into the bowl with the other ingredients and blend it well with a mixer.

Sift the coconut flour so it doesn't clump and add it to the other ingredients.

Again, use your mixer to thoroughly combine the ingredients. Make sure there are no lumps in the mix.

Add 1 mushed banana to the mix and combine it as well. This completes the muffin batter.

Put paper cups on a muffin tin and scoop the muffin batter into paper cups. Typically, I use 3 tbs of batter for this.

Add 7-9 blueberries on top of each muffin and push them down slightly into the batter. Don't press them two deep or into folds of the batter, or they will end up inside the muffins during baking.

Bake the muffins at 325°F (160°C) for about 45 minutes. To test if they are done, you can insert a toothpick in the middle and see if it comes out clean.

Remove the muffins from the oven and let them cool.

Enjoy!

Beverages

These are only a few of the recipes I use myself. I have written a whole book filled only with my coconut and fruit-vegetable smoothies that I personally use for fitness and after practicing kung fu. You can find it by clicking here.

1. Coconut Protein Smoothie

10-12 **ice cubes**
1 cup of **water**
1-2 tbs **protein powder** (optional)
3 tbs **coconut milk**
3 tbs **coconut flour**
1 tbs **flax seeds** (ground)
1 tbs pure **vanilla extract**

Simply place all of the ingredients in a blender and process it at high speed until the mix is well combined. Depending on how cold you want the smoothie to be, you may need to use more or less ice cubes.

Enjoy!

2. Tropical Coconut Smoothie

10-12 **ice cubes**
3 tbs **coconut oil** (melted)
1 tbs **coconut flour**
2 tbs **organic honey**
1 cup fresh **strawberries** (sliced)
1 **banana** (peeled, mashed)
1 cup **pineapple chunks**
2 **kiwis** (peeled, halved)
2 large **mangoes** (peeled, diced)

Combine the coconut oil, coconut flour and mashed banana in a small bowl. Mix these ingredients thoroughly.

Pour the mixture into a blender and add the other ingredients on the list except for the ice cubes.

Blend the mixture at high speed until it is well blended.

Add the ice and blend until all of the ice is crushed.

Enjoy!

3. Mango Strawberry Coco Drink

10-12 ice **cubes**
1 ½ cups **coconut milk**
4 **egg yolks**
1-2 tbs **coconut oil** (melted)
1 tbs **honey** (optional)
1 cup frozen or fresh **strawberries**
1 cup frozen or fresh **mangos**
1 tbs **vanilla extract**
1 dash **sea salt**

Blend the coconut milk, egg yolks, coconut oil and honey (optional) until the mixture is smooth.

Add the remaining ingredients and blend everything until it is smooth as well.

Enjoy!

4. Cocoa Coco Drink

Did I ever mention how healthy pure cocoa is? Milk chocolate is not healthy, but dark bitter chocolate is, because it contains so much cocoa. Therefore, here is a healthy treat for you, if you ever want one.

1 tbs **coconut oil**
1 tbs **cocoa powder**
1 pinch **salt**
¼ tsp organic **whole sugar** (optional)

Boil water and pour it into a mug. Let it sit for 30 seconds. Empty the water and put the coconut oil in the empty cup. The oil will quickly melt into a liquid.

Add the cocoa powder and salt to the oil and stir the mix.

Since cocoa is bitter, add the organic sugar.

Pour boiling water in the cup and stir.

Enjoy!

Note: I have also done this drink adding a bit of honey or coconut milk.

5. Popeye's Power Smoothie

This recipe is very dear to me, because I got it as a boy from Malin, my Tokelauan friend who originally introduced me to coconuts.

10 **ice cubes** (optional)
1 handful whole **spinach leaves**
1 tbs whole golden **flax seed**, ground
1 scoop **mint antioxidant Omega 3 greens**
1 - 2 cups **raw milk** or **coconut milk**
1 **banana** (peeled, sliced into chunks)
1 tsp **coconut oil** (melted)

Simply combine these ingredients in a blender and blend them until they are smooth. If you don't add the ice cubes, it will be a pretty thick smoothie.

Enjoy!

6. Eggnog-Coconut Smoothie

1 ½ cups **coconut milk**
2 tbs **coconut oil** (melted)
2 tbs **coconut cream** concentrate
5 soy-free **eggs**
½ tsp **nutmeg** (optional)
½ tsp **ginger** (ground)
½ tsp **cinnamon**
¼ tsp **salt**
4-5 **bananas**

Add all ingredients except for the bananas in a blender and blend them thoroughly.

Add the bananas and blend the mix until smooth.

Serve the smoothie with a sprinkle of nutmeg on top.

Enjoy!

7. Blueberry Coconut Smoothie

This is the simplest and yet one of the best smoothies I know.

10 **ice cubes**
¾ cup **coconut milk**
½ cup **blueberries**
½ **banana**
1 tbs **coconut oil**
2 tbs whole milk **plain yogurt**

Add everything except the ice cubes in a blender and blend it until the mixture is smooth.

Add the ice cubes at the end, if you wish, and blend them in as well.

Enjoy!

8. Vanilla Strawberry Smoothie

1-2 tbs **coconut oil** (melted)
2/3 cup **coconut milk** or **raw milk**
½ cup **plain yogurt**
1 ½ tsp **vanilla extract**
8 fresh or frozen **strawberries**

Except for the coconut oil, blend all ingredients in a blender. While the blender is running, slowly pour the coconut oil into it.

Pour the finished blend into a glass.

Optionally, add some dried coconut or a fresh strawberry.

Enjoy!

Meals

1. Vegetable Coconut Terrine

2 **garlic cloves** (minced)
1 tsp **salt**
1 pinch **pepper**
1 tsp **parsley** (minced)
1 tsp **oregano** (minced)
1 **bay leaf**
1 tsp **coconut oil**
1/8 tsp **nutmeg**
1 cup of **yellow onion** (in strips)
1 cup **squash** (in strips)
1 cup **zucchini** (in strips)
½ cup **green peas**
½ cup **coconut milk**
½ cup **coconut flakes**
½ **orange** (optional)

Preheat the oven at 390°F (200°C).

Mix the garlic, parsley, oregano, salt and nutmeg. Put the coconut oil either in a terrine or an oven proof dish.

Place the vegetables in the dish in alternate layers, sprinkling each layer with the spice mix from before.

Pour the coconut milk on top and sprinkle everything with the coconut flakes. Optionally, top with orange slices.

Cover the dish and bake until vegetables are tender. This should take about 15 minutes.

Enjoy!

2. Coconut Oil Stir Fry

For this recipe, use any organic meat you wish. I suggest using chicken.

1 tbs **coconut oil**
1 lb. (450 g) **organic meat** (cooked, chopped)
2 **eggs**
2 **carrots** (sliced)
2 bunches **collard** (sliced in strips)
2 **celery stalks** (sliced)
1 bunch **kale** (sliced in strips)
3 cups cooked **jasmine rice**
Organic fermented **soy sauce**

Melt the coconut oil in a large frying pan over medium heat.

Stir fry the meat until browned.

Add the eggs and stir while cooking.

Add carrots and fry them until very slightly tender.

Add the celery and continue stirring.

Add chopped kale and collards.

Fry everything for a few minutes before adding the rice. Continue frying and stirring for 6 - 9 minutes.

Serve with organic fermented soy sauce.

Enjoy!

3. Coconut Rice Meal

1 ¾ cup **coconut milk**
1 tbs **coconut oil**
¼ cup **water**
1 cup **coconut flakes**
1 cup **basmati rice**

Combine coconut milk, oil and water in a pot and bring it to a slow boil.

Add the rice and coconut flakes to the pot and bring it back to a boil, then turn the heat down to simmer and cover the pot with a lid, leaving it slightly ajar for steam to escape.

After 10 minutes, stir briefly.

Let it cook until the rice is tender.

Add more water and coconut milk if needed.

Fluff the rice and serve.

Note: This meal goes well with seafood.

Enjoy!

4. Artistic Coconut Soup

Basically, this is a soup that changes every time I make it, depending on which ingredients I have at hand. This is why I call it my artistic soup, because it is not so much a recipe as a placeholder for variability, for experimentation and a whole lot of serendipity. Sometimes, you can create fantastic new recipes this way. Here's one that I like.

4 cups **chicken broth** or **beef broth**
1 **red potato** (diced)
2 small **carrots** (chopped)
2 ribs **celery** (chopped)
½ **yellow onion** (chopped)
Lemon pepper or **black pepper**
Salt to taste
2 - 4 tbs **coconut oil**
Handful **herb salad mix**
1 small + 1 medium **zucchini** (diced)
3 large cloves **garlic** (minced)
2 knob **ginger** (peeled, minced)
Juice of ½ **lemon**

Bring the broth to a boil.

Whatever your exact ingredients are, first add the vegetables that need to cook longer. For example, add the potatoes first and boil them for a few minutes. Then add celery, onions and carrots. You can add seasoning at this point or at the end. If you want carrots only partly cooked, at them in the last 5-10 minutes.

Lower heat and simmer for 25-30 minutes or until the potatoes are tender, if you have them in your ingredient list.

5. Banana-Coco Bread

While I swear on coconut oil and bananas *on* bread, this is bread partially *made* from these ingredients.

2 tsp **baking powder**
½ tsp **baking soda**
3 cups **wheat flour**
½ tsp **salt**
2 cups **sugar**, or to taste (optional)
1 cup **coconut oil**
4 **eggs** (lightly beaten)
4 tsp **vanilla extract**
2 **bananas** (mashed)
1 cup **coconut cream**
1 cup **shredded coconut** (optional)
1 cup **walnuts** or **cashews** (optional, chopped)

Preheat your oven to 325°F (200°C).

In a bowl, combine baking powder, flour, baking soda and salt. Set it aside. In another bowl, combine vanilla extract, sugar, eggs, coconut oil, bananas and coconut cream.

Stir the coconut mixture until it is one slightly moist paste. Optionally, add shredded coconut and nuts.

Pour everything into two greased and floured loaf pans. Size: 8 ½ inch by 4 ½ inch by 2 ½ inch. In metric units, this is 22 cm by 12 cm by 6.5 cm.

Bake it in the oven for 1 hour. Let them cool for 10 minutes in the pans before taking them out and putting them to a wire rack to cool off completely.

Note: When it's fresh, this bread can be eaten without anything on it. Remember, it already has banana and coconut in it!

6. Gluten Free Coco Pancakes

½ tsp **baking powder**
2 **eggs**
2 tbs **coconut oil** (melted)
1 tsp **sugar** (optional)
¼ cup **heavy cream**
1 pinch of **salt**
¾ cup **shredded coconut**

Add the eggs, heavy cream, coconut oil, optional sugar and salt in a bowl.

In another bowl, mix the baking powder and shredded coconut.

Add both together and mix gently until it is a completely mixed batter.

Melt the coconut oil in a frying pan over medium heat.

Spoon the batter into the pan, making one or two circles at a time. Make sure the pancakes don't touch each other.

Fry them until the edges start to frill and get brown, then flip them gently and fry the second side for another minute.

Remove the pancakes to a dish and enjoy them immediately as you would traditional pancakes.

Note: If you cover them with a plastic wrap, you can put leftover pancakes in the fridge. However, they won't be as fluffy as fresh pancakes when you take them back out.

Enjoy!

7. Grainless Coco Rolls

1/3 cup **coconut flour**
1 **egg**
1 tsp **honey**
¼ cup **arrowroot powder**
1 tsp **sea salt**
½ cup **water**
1 cup **tapioca starch**
½ cup **coconut oil** (melted)
1 tbs **poppy seeds** (optional)
½ tsp **garlic powder** (optional)
1 tbs **sesame seeds** (optional)

Preheat oven to 350°F (180°C).

Put all dry ingredients in a bowl and whisk to combine them.

In another bowl, combine the egg, honey, water and coconut oil.

Add the liquid ingredients to the dry ones and mix everything until it is well combined.

Divide the dough into 8 parts and roll each of them into a ball. As you are doing this, use additional arrowroot powder to keep the dough from sticking to your fingers.

Optionally, combine Sesame seeds, poppy seeds and garlic powder in a separate bowl. Lightly roll each ball in the seed mixture. Line a baking sheet with unbleached parchment paper and place each ball on it.

Reduce oven temperature to 325°F (160°C) and place the baking sheet on the middle rack. Bake for about 40 minutes. Let the balls cool off after taking them out.

Enjoy!

8. Lemon Coco-Broco

This is a quick and healthy broccoli meal that I like to eat after working out harder than usual.

1 bunch **broccoli**
3 cloves **garlic** (sliced)
½ **lemon**
1 tbs **coconut oil** (melted)
Salt and **pepper** to taste

Preheat your oven to 425°F (220°C).

Break the broccoli up into florets.

Pour the melted coconut oil over the broccoli and garlic, then mix them.

Place the mix on a sheet pan and sprinkle it with salt and pepper.

Roast it until broccoli is tender. This should not take longer than 20 minutes. Remove the broccoli from the oven and sprinkle it with lemon juice.

Enjoy!

9. Coconut Turkey Stuffing

2-4 tbs **coconut oil**
¼ cup **coconut butter** or **regular butter**
1-2 stalks **celery** (chopped)
½ **onion** (diced finely)
½ tsp **sage**
½ tsp **rosemary**
½ tsp **thyme**
½ tsp **marjoram**
Salt and **pepper** to taste
4 cups **chicken stock**
6 cups dried **bread cubes**
1 **egg** (beaten)

Preheat oven to 350°F (180°C).

Melt the coconut oil and butter in a frying pan over medium heat.

Add onion and celery. Sauté until the onion is soft.

Add seasonings and the chicken stock. Heat it until it is warm.

Put the bread cubes in a large bowl and pour the chicken stock over it. Stir to mix it, while the bread soaks up all the liquid.

Add a beaten egg to it and mix it well.

Put the stuffing in a greased glass pan and bake it in the oven for 20-30 minutes. Take it out of the oven, let it cool a bit and stuff the turkey with it.

Note: For a gluten free stuffing, choose gluten free bread.

Enjoy.

Salads

1. Coco Chicken Curry Salad

1 tbs **coconut cream**, or to taste
Salt and **pepper** to taste
1 tbs **curry powder**
2 tbs **sour cream** or **yogurt**
1 **sweet apple** (chopped)
2 **green onions** (chopped)
2 tbs **shredded coconut**
1 handful **pecans** or **cashews** (chopped)
1 organic **chicken breast** (cooked, shredded)
Salad greens of your choice

Combine the coconut cream, curry powder, sour cream, salt and pepper in a medium sized bowl.

Stir the ingredients until they are combined.

Add the remaining ingredients and pour everything over the salad greens of your choice.

Note: The mix can also be used as a sandwich spread.

2. Coconut Pineapple Salad

2 cups fresh or canned **pineapple** (diced)
½ cup **shredded coconut**
1 tbs **arrowroot powder**
½ cup **sour cream** or **yogurt**
1 - 2 tbs **honey**, to taste
1 tsp **vanilla extract**
Pecans (optional)

In a bowl, mix the sour cream or yogurt, vanilla extract, honey and arrowroot powder together.

Add shredded coconut and pineapple to the bowl and stir.

Let the coconut and pineapple soak in the mix fluid to allow the flavors to blend. Optionally, if time is no issue, you can put it in a refrigerator and let it marinate for 2 hours. This is for maximum results.

Optionally, sprinkle the mix with chopped pecans or cashews just before serving.

Enjoy!

3. Pasta Coconut Salad

This can either be seen as a meal or noodle salad, depending on whether you let everything cool at the end or eat it warm.

4 tbs **coconut oil**
2-3 cloves **garlic** (minced)
Shredded coconut
½ cup **red onion** (diced)
¼ cup **yellow bell pepper** (diced)
¼ cup **green bell pepper** (diced)
¼ cup **red bell pepper** (diced)
1 lb. (450 g) **penne pasta** (cooked)
¼ cup sun dried **tomatoes in olive oil** (chopped)
½ cup **basil** (chopped)
Salt and **pepper** (optional)
Grated **parmesan cheese**

Make sure you have the pasta cooked by the end, so either cook it first or try to get it done at the same time.

Melt the coconut oil in a medium sized frying pan. Add both garlic and onion and stir them together. Add all of the peppers and basil.

Cook the mix until it is tender. Add the contents of the pan to your cooked pasta and stir everything together with sun dried tomatoes.

Optionally, season it with salt and pepper and top with parmesan cheese. Finally, add shredded coconut.

For salad, let it cool off for a while and then put it in the fridge. For a meal, eat it hot.

4. Sautéed Carrot Salad

This one is quick and simple, if time is short or a small hunger creeps up on you. I use this one to get the healthy dose of carrots I want in my diet.

5-6 large **carrots**
1 large **yellow onion**
2 tsp **coconut oil**
1 pinch **salt** to taste (optional)

Wash and cut the carrots into julienne strips. Slice onion into thin rings.

Melt coconut oil in a frying pan. Sauté the carrots and onions over high heat until they are tender and browned.

Optionally, add salt to taste before serving.

Enjoy!

5. Nutty Coconut Granola

This recipe is perfect for the whole family and parties, as it yields 21-23 cups of granola and lasts quite some time before it's gone. It is flavorful and very nutritious. You can use it as a substitute for breakfast cereals, using almond milk.

6 cups **coconut flakes**
1 ½ cups **honey**
¼ cup **maple syrup**
1 cup **coconut oil**
1 tsp **nutmeg**
1 tbs **cinnamon**
1 tsp **salt**
1 tbs **vanilla extract**
2 cups **pecan** halves
2 cups **almonds**
2 cups **sunflower seeds**
1 ½ cups **walnuts**
2 cups **cashews**
½ cup raw **sesame seeds**
1 ½ cups **pumpkin seeds**
2 cups **flax seeds**

Combine all wet ingredients and all spices in a frying pan. Over low heat, warm the pan and stir to blend the flavors of the mix.

Chop the coconut flakes to the size of oats and add them to the pan. Turn off the heat.

Place the rest of your dry ingredients in a bowl and add the wet mix to it. Stir everything until it is well blended.

You can store the granola in an airtight container and it will keep for weeks, if need be.

6. Dinner Coco Salad

This salad goes well with a lot of dinners, particularly chicken.

1 tbs **tomato paste**
1 tbs **mustard**
1 tbs **coconut vinegar** or **apple cider vinegar**
1 tbs **coconut oil** (melted)
2 tbs **shredded coconut**
¼ cup **shredded raw cheese** (optional)
4 cups torn up **spinach**

Combine the tomato paste, mustard, vinegar and coconut oil in a large serving bowl and whisk them together.

Add the spinach, shredded coconut and optionally the cheese.

Enjoy!

7. Fruit Coconut Salad

½ cup **shredded coconut**
1 small **pineapple** (diced)
3 **bananas** (peeled, sliced)
2 cups **strawberries** (chopped)
2 cups **blueberries**

For the dressing
2 tbs **honey**
2 tbs **lime juice**
2 tsp **lemon zest**
4 tbs **coconut milk**

Preheat the oven to 350°F (180°C).

Place the shredded coconut on a baking sheet and bake it for about 5 minutes or until it starts to brown. Take it out and set it aside.

Combine all the fruits in a large serving bowl.

In a small mixing bowl, combine the dressing ingredients and whisk them together.

Pour the dressing over the fruit mix. Toss the mix a bit to properly coat it with the dressing.

Sprinkle it with the baked coconut and serve it.

Enjoy!

Chapter 6:
130 Applications of Coconut Oil

One of the best things about coconut oil is its versatility. For example, I keep a pot of coconut oil in my kitchen and in my bathroom, because the oil is not only good to eat, but also very good for your skin and hair.

Just imagine, if you use it as hand lotion in the morning, you can immediately touch your breakfast buns or fruits and eat them, because the lotion itself is an edible substance and not some artificial product.

The following list contains no less than 130 uses for coconut oil that I have either tested, come up with, been told or discovered in scientific papers. It is divided into several subsections and given in alphabetical order.

Applications for Personal Hygiene

1. Age Spots aka liver spots – application of coconut oil on age spots can help them fade.

2. After Shave – coconut oil is very good for your skin and has a natural coconut smell. You can use it as after shave. It supports skin regeneration and helps against razor burn.

3. Baldness – since coconut oil is known to support cell regeneration, you can apply it to a section of your scalp affected by hair loss. Apply two to three times a day.

4. Birth Marks – if you get birth marks removed via laser surgery, coconut oil will aid your skin to heal faster.

5. Bruise Relief – again, the skin healing effects of coconut oil come to the rescue, if you have suffered a bruise. Apply it

directly to the bruise and it will help to reduce redness and swelling.

6. Bug Stings and Bites – coconut oil won't keep mosquitoes and bugs away, but it helps to stop the itching and burning of your skin if they bite you.

7. Burns – if you get burned, apply coconut oil to the area until the injury has fully healed.

8. ChapStick Alternative – oh, how I hate those dry lips in winter. Coconut oil to the rescue: apply some to your lips and say adios to scrubby kisses.

9. Dandruff – apply coconut oil to your scalp to moisturize dry skin and relieve the symptoms of dandruff.

10. Deodorant – I discovered this while cooking. If you mix some coconut oil with arrowroot powder and baking soda, the result is a deodorant. Now that's serendipity!

11. Diaper Rash Salve – my sister told me about this one. She uses organic coconut oil as a natural rash salve, so she doesn't have to use something laden with chemicals on her baby.

12. Exfoliator – this is known to the Tokelauan people; friend Malin told me about it long ago. Mix coconut oil with sea salt and you get an exfoliator you can use everywhere on your body.

13. Eye Wrinkle Cream – coconut oil is good against wrinkles, so apply some under your eyes. Not only will it reduce wrinkles, but bags as well.

14. Hair Protection – I mentioned this before and I also read a scientific paper about this. Coconut oil protects the hair from losing proteins like nothing else, if you apply it before washing. In addition, you can use it as conditioner after you're done washing. A teaspoon of coconut oil is enough for long hair. Run your fingers through your hair to distribute the oil, then you can simply leave it in.

15. Healing – after an injury, applying coconut oil on the wound shields it against dust and microorganisms. Coconut oil also helps with the healing process, is free of chemicals and smells better than pharmaceutical products.

16. Lubricant – coconut oil can serve as a chemical free personal lubricant that even smells good.

17. Makeup Remover – this one comes from my sister. Simply use a cotton swab with a bit of melted coconut oil to remove makeup.

18. Massage Oil – an obvious application of coconut oil, yet it took me months before I realized it. I've been using it ever since.

19. Moisturizer – every day, a former classmate of mine used to moisturize her hands using a smelly lotion that gave me a headache. After I gave her some coconut oil to save myself, she started using it all the time and has been swearing on it ever since.

20. Nipple Remedy – coconut oil is not only good for dry lips, but also for sore or dry nipples due to breastfeeding.

21. Oily Skin Remedy – if you are suffering from oily skin like me, then the way to help reduce it is to apply a bit of coconut oil on your face. Sounds counterintuitive, but it works for me.

22. Pre-Shave – shaving always hurts a little, but if you use coconut oil beforehand, it prepares the skin and reduces damage.

23. Skin Problems – I have a young brother with atopic eczema. Coconut oil keeps the rashes and itching in check. It is not a cure, but it helps him quite a lot. Also applicable to other skin problems, like psoriasis or dermatitis.

24. Sun Burn Remedy – the Tokelauans have known this for a thousand years, given they are islanders in the south Pacific. Apply to sunburn for quick relief.

25. Sunscreen: you can buy natural coconut sunscreen. It has the additional quality of serving as a lotion at the same time.

26. Swimmer's Ear Remedy – this condition is also known as otitis externa. Simply mix coconut oil and garlic oil, then put two drops in the inflamed ear and leave it for around 10 minutes. Repeat this process 2-3 times a day to get rid of this condition. From what I gather, it works within 2 days.

27. Tattoo Rash Relief – getting a tattoo is a somewhat painful experience. The skin burns and needs to heal first, so using coconut oil will help.

28. Toothpaste Alternative – believe it or not, coconut oil and baking soda is a perfectly fine toothpaste. So if you ever run out of paste, simply use this as an alternative.

29. Wrinkle Reducer – coconut oil is known to reduce wrinkles and strengthen the skin. I already mentioned it for bags and wrinkles under the eyes, but it can be used for any wrinkles.

Applications for Wellness Benefits

30. Breastfeeding – for mothers, eating 3 tablespoons of coconut oil every day enriches the milk with its benefits.

31. Bones – coconut oil enhances bone development, because it helps the body to absorb magnesium and calcium.

32. Digestion – as mentioned earlier in the book, coconut oil helps the body against parasites and fungi that cause problems related to digestion. The saturated fatty acids in coconut oil not only aid in the absorption of magnesium and calcium for your bones, but also in the absorption of

vitamins, other minerals and amino acids. This leads to a general health improvement.

33. Energy Bomb – coconut oil contains a lot of calories (energy) and thus boosts your energy level and endurance. As a health nut and Kung Fu practitioner, I found that coconut oil is a great supplement not only for me, but athletes in general.

34. Fitness – coconut oil is not only an energy bomb, but it increases your metabolism and helps you to lose weight rather than gain it. This makes it ideal for fitness purposes as well.

35. Insulin – it has been shown that coconut oil can help with insulin secretion and the utilization of blood glucose. Because of this, coconut oil is great for diabetics.

36. Lung Function – according to the scientific papers I've been swimming through, coconut oil can increase the fluidity of cell surfaces and thus increases lung function.

37. Nose bleeds – people sensitive to extreme heat or cold can experience nose bleeds, due to the nasal passages getting so dry that the skin cracks. If this applies to you, coat your finger with some coconut oil and gently rub it in your nostrils.

38. Stress Relief – as it turns out, the natural coconut aroma of coconut oil is very soothing and has the capacity to lower stress levels. So if you are suffering from stress, apply coconut oil on your face like lotion. Not only is it beneficial to your skin, but the aroma will help you calm down.

39. Weight Loss – coconut oil has 90% medium- and small-chain saturated fats which are very easy to digest and turn into usable energy. This helps you lose weight, because it tells the brain that less food is required to meet the day's energy needs.

Applications for Your Health

By now you probably understand how the different applications of coconut oil work and what kind of benefits there are to play with. While I explained what to do in all the points above, I will only repeat myself if I continue to do that. Therefore, to save time and not be repetitive, I shall just name the benefit from this point on, unless there is something more to say.

40. Acid Indigestion Aid – if coconut oil is used after a meal.

41. Adrenal Fatigue

42. Allergies – such as hay fever

43. Alzheimer's and Dementia – it can help, but it doesn't heal the condition

44. Asthma – due to the aroma

45. Bowel Function

46. Bronchial Infections

47. Cancer – may help to prevent breast cancer, according to laboratory tests

48. Candida Albicans

49. Cholesterol Levels – coconut oil improves the ratio of good cholesterol (HDL) and bad cholesterol (LDL). Helpful for people with high cholesterol levels

50. Chronic Fatigue.

51. Circulation – increases circulation, if you feel cold a lot.

52. Colds and Flus

53. Constipation Remedy

54. Cystic Fibrosis

55. Depression – believe it or not, depression is an inflammatory disease. Curing it is easy. Coconut oil helps on the nutritional end of the problem, but you must also engage in brisk walking for 30 minutes, 3 times a week. This simple exercise has the same anti-depressant effects as drugs. You also need sunlight. If there is none, like in winter, get a 10000 lux light box on Amazon and use it every morning within 1 hour of waking up. After just 1 week, the depression will be gone, even if it is chronic. Trust me.

56. Dysentery

57. Edema

58. Fever Support

59. Gallbladder Disease and Pain

60. Gas

61. Helicobacter pylori

62. Head Lice

63. Heart Disease – coconut oil protects arteries from atherosclerosis

64. Hemorrhoids – apply internally or externally twice per day

65. HIV – very often, coconut oil is said to help with HIV. However, this is misinformation, as there are no conclusive studies on this. Maybe it helps somewhat, maybe it doesn't. But as always, it is no cure.

66. Hot Flashes

67. Hyperthyroidism

68. Immune System Builder

69. Irritable Bowel Syndrome – and other problems related to digestion

70. Jaundice

71. Kidney Disease

72. Kidney Stones – coconut oil can help dissolve kidney stones, but don't rely on it solely.

73. Fatty Liver Disease – a very common condition that everybody who drinks alcohol suffers from at least mildly. I even wrote a bestselling book on it, which you can find here. Coconut oil is a very good food to eat, if you have a fatty liver. For a complete nutrition plan, feel free to check out my book.

74. Lung Disease

75. Malnutrition

76. Mental Clarity

77. Menstruation Relief – coconut oil helps with cramps and heavy blood flow

78. Migraines – I used to suffer from migraines much more often before I started eating coconut oil regularly

79. Mononucleosis

80. Osteoporosis

81. Pancreatitis

82. Periodontal Disease and tooth decay

83. Prostate Enlargement

84. Rickets

85. Scurvy

86. Stomach Ulcers

87. Thrush

88. Thyroid Function

89. Ulcerative Colitis

90. Urinary Tract Infections

Applications on Your Body

91. Acne

92. Athlete's Foot

93. Back Pain and Sore Muscles

94. Boils and Cysts

95. Canker Sores

96. Cellulite

97. Decongestant – when you are congested from a cold or allergies like hay fever, simply rub the coconut oil below your nose.

98. Ear Infection – put two or three drops of melted coconut oil in your ear twice a day in order to experience pain relief. It also help to fight the infection.

99. Gum Disease and Gingivitis – easiest if you use coconut oil as toothpaste.

100. Herpes

101. Hives

102. Pink Eye

103. Toothache – according to my little brother, it works.

104. Warts

Applications in the Kitchen

105. Butter and Margarine Substitute – a 1 to 1 substitute and much healthier than margarine.

106. Nutritional Supplement – add to smoothies in melted form, like in the recipes I give in chapter 4.

107. Oil substitute – replace oils you use for baking, cooking and sautéing with coconut oil.

Applications for Pets

Note: The rule of thumb for the dosage is 1/4 teaspoon per pound of body mass, given twice a day. For example, 8 pounds means 8 * 1/4 = 2 teaspoons.

108. Arthritis and Ligament Problems

109. Bad Breath Remedy

110. Cuts, Wounds, Stings, Bites – promotes healing.

111. Digestion and Nutrient Absorption

112. Disinfection

113. Dry Skin

114. Eliminates hairballs and reduces coughing

115. Energy – helps sedentary dogs to have more energy.

116. Fur Quality – makes fur shiny and glossy.

117. General health – Add coconut oil to their food daily.

118. Hair Protection

119. Old Dogs – old dogs have an amyloid buildup in their brain, which causes brain lesions. The Medium-chain triglycerides (MCTs) in coconut oil increase brain energy metabolism and decrease the amyloid buildup.

120. Skin Conditions, Flea Allergies and Itchiness

121. Yeast and fungal Infections

122. Weight Loss – our cat used to be a bit overweight.

General Applications of Coconut Oil

123. Chewing Gum Removal – if you ever have the misfortune of having chewing gum in your hair, there now is a way to get it out without cutting. Rub coconut oil over the gum, leave it for half an hour, then roll the gum between your fingertips and it should come off.

124. Insect Repellent – coconut oil itself often attracts insects, because of its high nutritional value. However, if you mix coconut oil and peppermint oil extract, it repels insects better than chemical products designed to do just that. Much saver and cheaper.

125. Leather Cleaning and Moisturizing

126. Polish Metals – you can use coconut oil to polish metals and deepen the color of bronze. Simply rub a little oil into a cotton towel and use it to wipe.

127. Polish Furniture – for wood furniture, you can mix coconut oil with a bit of lemon juice. I like it, but my sister doesn't, so better test it somewhere to see if it works for you.

128. Seasoning Animal Hide Drums

129. Seasoning Cookware

130. Soap Making – as mentioned earlier in the book, coconut oil is used as an ingredient in many lotions and soaps. You can also make soap from it yourself.

Conclusion

As you have seen, the false villain of the nineties is indeed a hero. Coconuts and their oil rank among the healthiest foods available on planet Earth and should be part of everyone's diet.

We know today that the processed foods of our civilization are the real threat to our bodies. Even if you eat the right foods, they will do you harm if they are processed and hence poisoned with trans fats and chemicals.

But there are good news. At the end of 2013, the American National Food and Drug Administration declared that enough scientific evidence has been brought forth in the past decades that trans fats are to disappear from our foods. There is no doubt in my mind that this step is going to lead to a healthier future for us all, since the rest of the world will eventually follow.

My advice to give you on your way is the following:

Don't go on a diet, instead have a good diet. Don't force your body, instead team up with it and give it healthy, organic, unprocessed foods. Dieting, that is fasting, causes eating disorders.

The human brain does most of its work behind the scenes. It knows how much weight your body is supposed to have. If you go on a diet, your brain thinks there is famine and you are starving. It will regulate your metabolism and hunger automatically and eventually bring you back to what it considers to be your healthy normal weight. This is why diets don't last.

Eat only when you are hungry and stop when you are full, not once your plate it empty. Better yet, stop when you are still a bit hungry, because the stomach is slow and doesn't react quickly enough to tell the brain that it has had enough.

Research has shown that if food is readily available, we experience more hunger and eat more. Don't overload the table with too much food, and don't keep food in visual range all day long.

I wish you good health.

Patrick Smith

Appendix: References

If you are not in the sciences, let me quickly explain what this section is about. In all proper research, it is obligatory that you cite the scientific sources of information that your research paper, article or books used or touched on. As a good scientist, when I studied the effects of coconut oil, I assembled a list of all the papers I went through. Below, you find this list.

Almost all scientific journals out there are pay-only and quite expensive. If you are at a university, you should have free access to most of these papers from the computers on your campus. This is because universities pay for membership in most journals, so any of their researchers and students can use them.

General Research on Coconut Oil

Dietary fatty acids and oxidative stress in the heart mitochondria. Mitochondrion. 2010 Aug 5.

Effects of Dietary Coconut Oil on the Biochemical and Anthropometric Profiles of Women Presenting Abdominal Obesity Lipids. 2009 May 13.

In vitro antimicrobial properties of coconut oil on Candida species in Ibadan, Nigeria.
J Med Food. 2007 Jun; 10(2):384-7.

Beneficial effects of virgin coconut oil on lipid parameters and in vitro LDL oxidation.
Clin Biochem. 2004 Sep; 37(9):830-5.

Coconut Oil Attenuates the Effects of Amyloid-β on Cortical Neurons In Vitro. J Alzheimers Dis. 2013 Oct 22.

Dietary coconut oil increases conjugated linoleic acid-induced body fat loss in mice independent of essential fatty acid deficiency.

Biochim Biophys Acta. 2005 Oct 15; 1737(1):52-60. Epub 2005 Sep 13.

Successful treatment of acute aluminium phosphide poisoning: possible benefit of coconut oil.
Hum Exp Toxicol. 2005 Apr; 24(4):215-8.

Coconut Oil Enhances Tomato Carotenoid Tissue Accumulation Compared to Safflower Oil in the Mongolian Gerbil (Meriones unguiculatus). J Agric Food Chem. 2012 Aug 16.

Choice of cooking oils–myths and realities.
J Indian Med Assoc 1998 Oct; 96(10):304-7

Wound management with coconut oil in Indonesian folk medicine, Chirurg 2002 Apr; 73(4):387-92

Energy restriction with high-fat diet enriched with coconut oil gives higher UCP1 and lower white fat in rats.
Int J Obes Relat Metab Disord. 1998 Oct; 22(10):974-9.

The role of coconut and coconut oil in coronary heart disease in Kerala, south India. Trop Doct. 1997 Oct; 27(4):215-7.

Coconut oil compound may treat STDs
AIDS Patient Care STDS 1999 Sep; 13(9):572

Dietary Conjugated Linoleic Acid Induces Lipolysis in Adipose Tissue of Coconut Oil-Fed Mice but not Soy Oil-Fed Mice.
Lipids. 2011 Jun 4

A diet rich in coconut oil reduces diurnal postprandial variations in circulating tissue plasminogen activator antigen and fasting lipoprotein (a) compared with a diet rich in unsaturated fat in women. J Nutr. 2003 Nov; 133(11):3422-7.

Cholesterol, coconuts, and diet on Polynesian atolls: a natural experiment: the Pukapuka and Tokelau island studies.
Am J Clin Nutr 1981 Aug; 34(8):1552-61

Intestinal adaptation in short bowel syndrome without tube feeding or home parenteral nutrition: report of four consecutive cases. Nutrition. 1998 Jun; 14(6):508-12.

Virgin Coconut Oil

Anti-inflammatory, analgesic, and antipyretic activities of virgin coconut oil.
Pharm Biol. 2010 Feb; 48(2):151-7.

Effect of virgin coconut oil enriched diet on the antioxidant status and paraoxonase 1 activity in ameliorating the oxidative stress in rats – a comparative study.
Food Funct. 2013 Jul 29

In vivo Antinociceptive and Anti-inflammatory Activities of Dried and Fermented Processed Virgin Coconut Oil
Med Princ Pract. 2011; 20(3):231-6. Epub 2011 Mar 29.

Hepatoprotective Activity of Dried- and Fermented-Processed Virgin Coconut Oil
Evidence-Based Complementary and Alternative Medicine Volume 2011 (2011), Article ID 142739

Virgin coconut oil supplementation prevents bone loss in osteoporosis rat model
Evid Based Complement Alternat Med. 2012; 2012:237236. Epub 2012 Sep 16.

An open-label pilot study to assess the efficacy and safety of virgin coconut oil in reducing visceral adiposity.
ISRN Pharmacol. 2011; 2011:949686. Epub 2011 Mar 15.

Wet and dry extraction of coconut oil: impact on lipid metabolic and antioxidant status in cholesterol coadministered rats.
Can J Physiol Pharmacol. 2009 Aug; 87(8):610-6

.

Beneficial effects of virgin coconut oil on lipid parameters and in vitro LDL oxidation. Clin Biochem. 2004 Sep; 37(9):830-5.

Antioxidant capacity and phenolic acids of virgin coconut oil. Int J Food Sci Nutr. 2009; 60 Suppl 2:114-23. Epub 2008 Dec

Effects Of Coconut Oil On Skin

Antimicrobial Property of Lauric Acid Against Propionibacterium Acnes: Its Therapeutic Potential for Inflammatory Acne Vulgaris. J Invest Dermatol. 2009 Apr 23

Novel antibacterial and emollient effects of coconut and virgin olive oils in adult atopic dermatitis.
Dermatitis. 2008 Nov-Dec

The effect of topical virgin coconut oil on SCORAD index, transepidermal water loss, and skin capacitance in mild to moderate pediatric atopic dermatitis: a randomized, double-blind, clinical trial. Int J Dermatol. 2013 Dec 10.

Development and Anti-microbial Potential of Topical Formulations Containing Cocos nucifera Linn.
Antiinflamm Antiallergy Agents Med Chem. 2013 Jun 4

Oil massage in neonates: an open randomized controlled study of coconut versus mineral oil.
Indian Pediatr. 2005 Sep; 42(9):877-84.

Effect of topical application of virgin coconut oil on skin components and antioxidant status during dermal wound healing in young rats.
Skin Pharmacol Physiol. 2010; 23(6):290-7. Epub 2010 Jun 3.

Uptake of vitamin E succinate by the skin, conversion to free vitamin E, and transport to internal organs.
Biochem Mol Biol Int. 1999 Mar; 47(3):509-18.

Effects Of Coconut Oil On Hair

Clinical trial showing superiority of a coconut and anise spray over permethrin 0.43% lotion for head louse infestation
Eur J Pediatr. 2010 Jan; 169(1):55-62.

Effect of mineral oil, sunflower oil, and coconut oil on prevention of hair damage.
J Cosmet Sci. 2003 Mar-Apr; 54(2):175-92

Secondary ion mass spectrometric investigation of penetration of coconut and mineral oils into human hair fibers: Relevance to hair damage. J Cosmet. Sci., 52, 169-184 (May/June 2001)

Research On Saturated Fats

Saturated fat is not the major issue
British Medical Journal, 2013 October 22, *347:f6340*

Dietary Fats and Health: Dietary Recommendations in the Context of Scientific Evidence
Advances in Nutrition, 2013 May 1; 4(3):294-302

Saturated fat prevents coronary artery disease? An American paradox, American Journal of Clinical Nutrition, Vol. 80, No. 5, 1102-1103, November 2004

Food Choices and Coronary Heart Disease: A Population Based Cohort Study of Rural Swedish Men with 12 Years of Follow-up
Int. J. Environ. Res. Public Health 2009, 6, 2626-2638

Results of use of metformin and replacement of starch with saturated fat in diets of patients with type 2 diabetes.
Endocr Pract 2002 May-Jun; 8(3):177-83

Meta-analysis of prospective cohort studies evaluating the association of saturated fat with cardiovascular disease. American Journal of Clinical Nutrition, 2010 Mar; 91(3):535-46.

Dietary fat intake and risk of stroke in male US healthcare professionals: 14 year prospective cohort study. BMJ. 2003 Oct 4; 327(7418):777-82

Research On Lauric Acid And Monolaurin

Glycerol monolaurate inhibits Candida and Gardnerella vaginalis in vitro and in vivo but not Lactobacillus. Antimicrob Agents Chemother. 2010 Feb; 54(2):597-601

Antibacterial study of the medium chain fatty acids and their 1-monoglycerides: individual effects and synergistic relationships. Pol J Microbiol. 2009; 58(1):43-7.

In Vitro Anti-Propionibacterium Activity by Curcumin Containing Vesicle System, Chemical and Pharmaceutical Bulletin (Tokyo). 2013; 61(4):419-25.

Effect of saturated fatty acid-rich dietary vegetable oils on lipid profile, antioxidant enzymes and glucose tolerance in diabetic rats. Indian J Pharmacol. 2010 Jun; 42(3):142-5.

Glycerol monolaurate prevents mucosal SIV transmission. Nature. 2009 Apr 23; 458(7241):1034-8.

Antimicrobial activity of potassium hydroxide and lauric acid against microorganisms associated with poultry processing. J Food Prot. 2006 Jul; 69(7):1611-5.

Effect of fatty acid chain length on suppression of ghrelin and stimulation of PYY, GLP-2 and PP secretion in healthy men. Peptides. 2006 Jul; 27(7):1638-43. Epub 2006 Mar 23.

Glycerol monolaurate inhibits virulence factor production in Bacillus anthracis. Antimicrob Agents Chemother. 2005 Apr; 49(4):1302-5.

Effect of fatty acids on arenavirus replication: inhibition of virus production by lauric acid
Arch Virol 2001; 146(4):777-90

Lauric acid inhibits the maturation of vesicular stomatitis virus. J Gen Virol. 1994 Feb; 75 (Pt 2):353-61.

Research On Medium Chain Triglycerides

Caprylic Triglyceride as a Novel Therapeutic Approach to Effectively Improve the Performance and Attenuate the Symptoms Due to the Motor Neuron Loss in ALS Disease
PLoS ONE 7(11): e49191. doi:10.1371/journal.pone.0049191 (2012)

Combined medium-chain triglyceride and chilli feeding increases diet-induced thermogenesis in normal-weight humans. Eur J Nutr. 2012 Nov 20.

Sophorolipid production by Candida bombicola on oils with a special fatty acid composition and their consequences on cell viability. Biotechnol Lett. 2010 Oct; 32(10):1509-14

Anti-bacterial and anti-inflammatory properties of capric acid against Propionibacterium acnes: A comparative study with lauric acid. J Dermatol Sci. 2013 Nov 7. pii: S0923-1811

Medium-chain Triglyceride Ketogenic Diet, An Effective Treatment for Drug-resistant Epilepsy and A Comparison with Other Ketogenic Diets. Biomed J. 2013 Jan; 36(1):9-15

Effect of ingestion of medium-chain triacylglycerols on moderate- and high-intensity exercise in recreational athletes.
J Nutr Sci Vitaminol (Tokyo). 2009 Apr; 55(2):120-5.

Partial replacement of dietary (n-6) fatty acids with medium-chain triglycerides decreases the incidence of spontaneous colitis in interleukin-10-deficient mice.
J Nutr. 2009 Mar; 139(3):603-10.

Inhibition of Candida mycelia growth by a medium chain fatty acids, capric acid in vitoro and its therapeutic efficacy in murine oral candidiasis Med Mycol J. 2012; 53(4):255-61.

Enhancement of muscle mitochondrial oxidative capacity and alterations in insulin action are lipid species dependent: potent tissue-specific effects of medium-chain fatty acids.
Diabetes. 2010 May; 59(5):1283.

Consumption of an oil composed of medium chain triacyglycerols, phytosterols, and N-3 fatty acids improves cardiovascular risk profile in overweight women.
Metabolism. 2003 Jun; 52(6):771-7.

Medium-Chain Oil Reduces Fat Mass and Down-regulates Expression of Adipogenic Genes in Rats.
Obes Res. 2003 Jun; 11(6):734-44.

An enteral therapy containing medium-chain triglycerides and hydrolyzed peptides reduces postprandial pain associated with chronic pancreatitis. Pancreatology. 2003; 3(1):36-40.

Medium-chain fatty acids improve cognitive function in intensively treated type 1 diabetic patients and support in vitro synaptic transmission during acute hypoglycemia.
 Diabetes. 2009 May; 58(5):1237-44.

Effects of beta-hydroxybutyrate on cognition in memory-impaired adults. (Applies to Alzheimer's)
Neurobiol Aging. 2004 Mar; 25(3):311-4.

Protective effects of medium-chain triglycerides on the liver and gut in rats administered endotoxin.
Ann Surg. 2003 Feb; 237(2):246-55.

Comparison of diet-induced thermogenesis of foods containing medium- versus long-chain triacylglycerols.
J Nutr Sci Vitaminol (Tokyo). 2002 Dec; 48(6):536-40.

Enteral nutrition in Crohn's disease: fat in the formula.
Eur J Gastroenterol Hepatol. 2003 Feb; 15(2):115-8.

Effects of intravenous supplementation with alpha-tocopherol in patients receiving total parenteral nutrition containing medium- and long-chain triglycerides. Eur J Clin Nutr 2002 Feb 56(2):121-8

Medium-chain triglycerides increase energy expenditure and decrease adiposity in overweight men.
Obes Res. 2003 Mar; 11(3):395-402.

Larger diet-induced thermogenesis and less body fat accumulation in rats fed medium-chain triacylglycerols than in those fed long-chain triacylglycerols.
J Nutr Sci Vitaminol (Tokyo). 2002 Dec; 48(6):524-9.

Protective effects of medium-chain triglycerides on the liver and gut in rats administered endotoxin.
Ann Surg. 2003 Feb; 237(2):246-55.

Value of VLCD supplementation with medium chain triglycerides.
Int J Obes Relat Metab Disord 2001 Sep; 25(9):1393-400

The influence of a preserved colon on the absorption of medium chain fat in patients with small bowel resection.
Gut. 1998 Oct; 43(4):478-83.

Killing of Gram-positive cocci by fatty acids and monoglycerides
APMIS 2001 Oct; 109(10):670-8

Physiological effects of medium-chain triglycerides: potential agents in the prevention of obesity.
J Nutr 2002 Mar; 132(3):329-32

Effects of different lipid sources in total parenteral nutrition on whole body protein kinetics and tumor growth. JPEN J Parenter Enteral Nutr. 1992 Nov-Dec; 16(6):545-51

In vitro killing of Candida albicans by fatty acids and monoglycerides. Antimicrob Agents Chemother 2001 Nov; 45(11):3209-12

Decreased fat and nitrogen losses in patients with AIDS receiving medium-chain-triglyceride-enriched formula vs those receiving long-chain-triglyceride-containing formula. Am Diet Assoc. 1997 Jun; 97(6):605-11

Enhanced thermogenesis and diminished deposition of fat in response to overfeeding with diet containing medium chain triglyceride. Am J Clin Nutr. 1982 Apr; 35(4):678-82

11481656R00046

Printed in Great Britain
by Amazon.co.uk, Ltd.,
Marston Gate.